Tea in Heliopolis

TEA IN
HELIOPOLIS

Poems

Hedy Habra

Press 53

Winston-Salem

Press 53, LLC
PO Box 30314
Winston-Salem, NC 27130

First Edition

SILVER CONCHO POETRY SERIES

Cover design by Paul Sizer

Cover art, "Tea in Heliopolis," Copyright © 2012 by Hedy Habra

Author photo by Michael T. Lanka

Printed on acid-free paper
ISBN 978-1-935708-76-6

Acknowledgments

Some of these poems have appeared, sometimes in a slightly different version in the following publications:

Alternatebridges.com, "Raindrops," "Transience"
Black Buzzard Review, "The Bullfrog"
Cutthroat: A Journal of the Arts, "Open-Air Cinema in Heliopolis"
Curbside Review, "Narguileh"
Fresh Ground, "It was Later on I Learned it was Harmless"
GraFemas, "Bricolage," "Simulacra"
Linden Lane Magazine, "Encounters," "Immured," "Waiting for Marie"
Mizna Literary Journal, "Raoucheh"
Museum Views: A Playhouse of the Muses, "Amber Daum"
Negative Capability, "A Glimpse of Fall," "Tea in Heliopolis," "That Day in Heliopolis," "Camera Lucida," "The White Brass Bed," "To Henriette"
Nimrod, "Lost and Found," "Tea at *Chez Paul's*"
The New York Quarterly, "Everything They Said"
Parting Gifts, "Salawat," "A Seaside Café, my First Taste of Fresh Oysters," "12 Rushdy Street," "The Road to Tyre," "Vision," "The Wheel," "Waves," "Your Name was Also Mary"
Pirene's Fountain, "To my Son Upon his First Trip to Lebanon"
Poet Lore, "First Bra," "*Mobilis in Mobili*"
Puerto del Sol, "How the Song Turns into a Legend," "Missing Words," "Waiting in a Field of Melted Honey"
The Smoking Poet, "*Adagio* for a Forgotten *Viola d'Amore*"
Sulphur River Review, "Milkweed"

ANTHOLOGIES

Come Together: Imagine Peace, eds. Larry & Ann Smith and Philip Metres (2008), "Blue Heron" (reprinted in *Encore*)
Inclined to Speak: Contemporary Arab American Poetry, ed. Hayan Charara (2008), "Black and White Photographs" (under different title), "Even the Sun has its Dark Side," "Milkweed" (reprinted from *Sulphur River Review* 1997), "Tea at *Chez Paul's*" (reprinted from *Nimrod* 2003)

AWARDS AND RECOGNITIONS

Letras Femeninas: Victoria Urbano Prize: First prize "Bricolage," "Simulacra" (2007)

Nimrod/Hardman Literary Award, Pablo Neruda Prize: Finalists: "Tea at *Chez Paul's*," "*Narguileh,*" "Open-Air Cinema in Heliopolis" (2003)

Pirate's Alley Faulkner Prize: Finalist: "*Raoucheh*" (1990)

Negative Capability's Eve of St. Agnes Award: Finalists: "A Glimpse of Fall" (1994); "To Henriette" (1993); "That Day in Heliopolis" (1992); "Tea at Heliopolis," "The White Brass Bed," "Camera Lucida" (formerly titled "Reflections") (1989)

Robert Writing Awards: "Transience," "Raindrops" (1990)

Linden Lane Magazine's Poetry Prize: First prize "Encounters" (1994); Third prize "Waiting for Marie" (1989); Finalist "Immured" (1987)

Tea in Heliopolis

I. Telling Her Story to Stray Dogs

II. Tea in Heliopolis

III. *Raoucheh*

IV. A Glimpse of Fall

I

Telling Her Story to Stray Dogs

Bricolage

Go every day a little deeper
into the woods, collect acorns,
twigs, thorns, fallen leaves,
pine needles, a fern's curl,
a bird's nest, a lost feather,
spring air, hot, humid air, a raindrop,
a touch of blue, a ripple,
and why not the hush
of your steps over moss,
the trembling of leaves
at dusk against black bark?

Put it all in a bag and shake it:
you will retrace your steps
within the clearing, hear frightened
flights, watch the rain darken the deck,
flatten oak leaves, answer the root's mute prayer.

Milkweed

Only at dusk is one swept by the deep
sweet scent of milkweed,
a turbulence
in the evening's crisp air. Scepters,
edging the road in triple rows,
crowned by pink,
minute star-like flowers
linked by invisible rays.

I pull the thick stem, an ancestral
gesture,
freeing hairy filaments
from rain-soaked earth, to bury
in the creek's
moist soil.
Rubbing my sticky fingers, I wonder
what powers lie
in the white bleeding
of broken leaves, the stigmata of purple
veins, cures lost
with old shamans,
before this land was named Michigan.

And I think of Lebanon, the green figs
we grew in the mountains
of Baabdat,
figs picked, children climbing forbidden
fences. At the bottom of each fig,
a white tear
covered the circular scar,
a tear, beading from invisible pores,
sheathing our skin
with transparent gloves.

I hear my mother's voice, an echo
of ancient wisdom,
purification rites:
"Never rub your eyes before washing
or you'll go blind!" Would milkweed
sap heal
sightless eyes, unaware
of star-like flowers
offering their last silk-winged seed?

A swarm of bees milks intangible beads;
I inhale the dizzying
scent, anchoring
myself in increasing darkness. A spark
reveals hidden berries,
the whiteness
of a Daisy, Queen Ann's lace,
fireflies,
springing from nowhere,
greener in a darkened back alley
between three black

trunks, rising motes of flame
in the cool liminal hour,
vision inside vision,
inside me, at the verge of the night,
the wild dance
of heated elytra
everywhere around grass and wildflower,

attentive only to that mysterious,
incoherent language,
emerging from folds
of bark, creased blades of grass,
moisture trapped
in lichen, in humus,
underneath blackened oak leaves.

Telling Her Story to Stray Dogs

She lay countless nights, her moans muffled by a pillow.
She could see his face that Summer morning, feel his voice bite
        into her flesh, a surgeon's scalpel, excising. She recalled
waking from a deep sleep, opening her door to the early,
        unannounced messenger, his words, burning like dry
ice. She stood motionless as he turned away, climbing hurriedly
        into his Honda. She felt a lightness, a readiness to levitate.
Looking down, she saw herself in shattered glass, concealing
        the Venetian red-tiled corridor like snow flakes. Folded
in two, she gathered some fragments, then for hours swept floors
        and corners filled with impalpable dust.

She was surprised to hear her heartbeat. "It must have
been my soul," she thought, "disintegrating into feathers of glass
        all over the house. It's flown everywhere, for everyone to see,
for everyone to blow away, broken debris coming out of nowhere."
        Weeks after, amianthus-like particles still shone on the sofas,
the afghans, the lace curtains, the oak rocker, the crease of a silk
        pillow, the fold of a diphenbachia leaf. Many months later,
sun rays would light insidiously a dark corner, reveal a faceted
        web of slivered dust, a glimmer on the edge of a window,
within the braided arm of a wicker chair.

The last one to bed, she'd lie, eyes open. Eating less each
day, she became paler, watched her mother stab the eye of round
        with a kitchen knife, saw how she pressed garlic cloves deep
into openings and brought edges together to mend the surface. At
        the dinner table no one would know the sealed roast had
been pierced in so many places. Now her wound had healed. In
        the long waking hours, she'd hear the doorbell ring, see
his words gather, needles welding into a silver scimitar. She could
        replay its swift movement in slow motion, fragment it all night-
long, fingers running over her side, redesigning the leaf's imprint.

She prayed for snow, for snow to cover his footsteps
around her house, around the fig and cherry trees, erasing their
traces for miles in the neighborhood, for snow to smother
and bury their geography of familiar places. And snow fell relentlessly
that Winter, and Spring was late, disconcerted. Snow
covered red-tiled roofs, cars, shrubs, rhododendrons, bird baths,
statues of Manneken Pis, the Virgin of Lourdes, the Virgin
of Guadalupe, even fir trees and hedges. Snow muffled voices
freezing the wind brushing the Lebanese Cedar hills, concealing
old carcasses, broken bones, ruins, the palace of *Beit el Habib*,
the central square's Martyrs' monument, bazaars, flakes shrouding
laced arcades, façades riddled with lead graffiti, abandoned rubble.

Lulled by the vast whiteness, she no longer yearned for the
change of seasons, but wished to dream again. Each morning,
folded in two, she would walk bent, smoothing the scar on her
side as if ironing a shrunken garment. At night, she'd hear a
crisscross, particles sliding against each other with each
move. Slowly, out of her falling eyelids, a silent, wordless presence
rocked her in a bed of rose petals. Soon, lost snow flakes
would melt into dew, avenues smell of lavender and tender
blossoms. She dreamed of roaming the streets, a village fool
telling her story to stray dogs, to leaves in the trees, chasing
the ones flying in the wind.

Tea at *Chez Paul's*

We ate Schtengels at *Chez Paul's*,
twisted breads sprinkled with coarse salt
      clinging to our lips.
We could see the sea enfolding us
through the tall bay windows
of the semi-circular Swiss teahouse.
You described a Phoenician Tale
just for me,
how the mountain slopes
reddened each spring
      with Adonis' blood,
how this delicate flower,
truly and duly Lebanese
has come to be called a red poppy, an anemone,
with all its melodious variations,
      alkhushkhash,
          un amapola,
             un coquelicot,
                ed anche un papavero...

We walked through a field scattered
with red poppies bright as when Ishtar
sprinkled nectar
on her beloved's blood.
      Time seemed elastic then,
          space infinite.
I wished to bring home a handful of scarlet light,
to keep the softness of its wrinkled petals
alive a while longer.
The moment I cut Adonis' flower,
hanging like a broken limb, its corolla fell over my hand,
head too heavy with dreams.
      No wonder blossoms tremble
          on their fragile stem.

Sometimes love is only real when not uprooted.
       Isn't there a geography of every emotion?
Not a precious, intricate *Carte du Tendre*,
       but a trail of forgotten footsteps mapping
every heartbeat, every motion?
             A stairwell, a car, a booth, a parking lot,
      a streetlight, a gateway,
an old-fashioned réverbère,
      a Bus Stop or maybe a tree, a tree stump,
a moss-covered path, a pond,
      a small creek, a flat stone,
         a hill, a porch or even a wooden bench?

Take the poppy, for instance. It will only breathe
and give joy at its birthplace.
       I can still feel the small flower melting
into liquid silk in my palm.
       I held the red petals to my cheek
like a morning kiss while you kept telling how Ishtar
         or as some may say Astarte, often mistaken for Isis,
            was truly her Phoenician incarnation,
before she was ever called Aphrodite or Venus.
       I remember how you talked and talked
until we both stepped into Ishtar's temple.

How the Song Turns into a Legend

We all have but one song, spend a lifetime
        looking for ways to say it,
            as one recites an unending poem,
a *chanson de geste*,
        a canto, or an epic.
What happens then if you whisper it only to yourself,
        burying it deeper every day?
            Wouldn't it wilt as petals pressed
between the pages of a book?
        And couldn't a garden die of indifference?

But take any couple, an encounter, turn it into a legend,
        make it last... Their story told and retold,
           ritualized by repetition,
until their stature grows, their eyes brighten,
        until their voice is heard,
            their sin forgiven...
Recount tales in tongues, in parables, uttered in public squares,
        whispered in corners
          in *sotto voce*,
            from mouth to mouth,
hear a mother's voice warn her children
           with a half-smile,
        witness puppets parody star-crossed lovers in street fairs,
        in jest, in awe,
in ever-changing roles and settings.

Watch words form lines, notes, scripts, scores written in scrolls,
        in parchment, in manuscripts folded in folio,
        in quarto,
scribbled in notebooks, in recipe books,
        in brown paper, engraved in stone, in bronze,
        gold or ivory,
           transcribed,
            transformed,

until only names are left untouched.
When so many variations deafen the original song,
then, and only then,
the images retain their spell,
become universal,
art legitimizing what could never endure.

Missing Words

We both stared at the illuminated images
of what must have been a rare book. Its pages
seemed to turn on their own, one by one,
following the rhythm of our breath—*were we so afraid
to touch its precious leaves?*

I noticed faded characters here and there, like
distant memories, missing lines rubbed away by fingers
or written in invisible ink, perhaps words never said,
unable to fall in proper order—*could the writer or scribe
have wished to light a match, imagined its fire racing along the
elongated curves of the phrase, erasing even the traces
of his thought?*

Then came an empty page, papyrus-like, arresting,
intimidating the one about to stamp it with the colors
of life—*what ever happened to this page, I wondered,
realizing you were gone*

A Seaside Café, My First Taste of Fresh Oysters

Was it Beirut or Alexandria?
Under the shade, you put aside
your Safari hat on an empty chair,
squeezed lemon over the moist flesh.
"Take all the juice," you said,
holding the iridescent
shell to my lips.

Yet one day you chased me
around the house, menacing,
a slipper in your raised hand.
No one recalls what I had done.
I was never caught. Only nine
years of hide and seek
and you were gone.

I have searched for you, father,
in every man, placed letters
into the wrong urns.
First loves, impossible loves.
I recall that time when
I wished I were his wife
until I saw him hold his child.
I would have given my life
to be his daughter.

Vision

Now a mural,
the page stretches,
calling for paint,
brushes, a ladder.
Words with clipped wings
stumble,
scattered here and there,
clothes
thrown in haste
as you rush
into a lover's arms.
Two androgynous silhouettes
engage
in an elegant tango,
twist and turn,
limbs bent in unison.

Later, when light after light
has been put out,
when oak branches brush
roofs and windows, filling
the house with murmurs,
when every sound
is a menace,
you rest in inkwell darkness.
Feathers escape their cotton
prison, circle
like maddened fireflies
bonfire sparks,
you think of midnight
rides in a Felukah
along the glistening Nile,
of the way timid lovers
write ephemeral messages,
with their lighted cigarettes.

A cloud of down
fills the room,
schools of flashing fish
slither
on the walls of your waking.
Following a ray of moon,
you yearn
for a sliver of diamond,
reach for paper, pen, to keep
the vision alive,
but it melts into water, vanishes
as you hold on tight to your
feather pillow.

To Henriette

Back to the house in Heliopolis,
wallpapered with oils, your oils. Were
they Renoir, Boucher, Monet, Manet,
Turner or Bouguereau? So many, you
forgot the artists' names. "I painted it
from a postcard," you'd say, or "a picture
my Art teacher gave me. It was so long
ago. Before I married your father."

I see you on the balcony, bent over
the easel, the crisp blue Egyptian sky
filtering through wrought iron balustrades, lost
in other dreamers' visions, you recreate trips
along the European countryside, smoothing
haystacks under the young peasant girl.
An intimacy you never knew.

You carefully rearrange the mantilla
of the woman watching the sunset from her
window. An oval mirror reveals her concern:
Is her lover late? She fears she no longer
pleases him. Through the verandah, framed
by stone pillars entwined with vines, waning
golden corals tinge the dark waters.

Day after day you instill life, following
the master's brush strokes, adding a touch
of blush, redefining the lower lip, preserving
the airiness of the gauze lining her profile.
Her confidante, you hear her intimate thoughts,
enter her world, visit places you'd only
seen in print. At night, the easel rests in
the bedroom shared with your mother, a widow.

16

You dream the painter painting his model,
merging dreams, erasing distances. You sleep,
smiling, inventing happy endings, excusing
the lover's delay, convincing the reluctant father.

I see you mastering that tempest, redress
the sinking ship's reclining masts, and blown
sails. Day after day, you wait for the paint
to dry next to the original, long months
for the fierce waves to reflect the lightning
menacing the deck's flickering red lantern.

Does it matter if you forgot the artist's name
when you possessed part of his soul?
You say: "I don't remember anymore,"
then laugh at my wild guesses:
"We're very much alike you and I..."

*   *

"There's no such thing as true love," you'd
say, " the greatest passion melts like ice."
How I wanted you to be wrong. Your canvases'
message reaches me, muffled by time and
distance, as I paint stage butterflies pinned
by Degas or Turner's gilded Venetian sunsets.

Was it a prince standing opposite the beauty
by the stream, above the upright Steinway?
Seated on a rock, her lower back loosely draped
in muslin, unabashed, she offers him her nudity,
turning towards us, eyes lowered, a perfect
profile. *Myosotis* crown her coiled hair,

a few falling, opalescent, over the nape of her
neck. The youth's belt encrusted with precious
gems, his heavily ornate chain and medallion,
a sign he is not a mere hunter. One hand raised,
he addresses the nymph, ceremoniously.

A child, I thought him her older brother,
reproaching her carelessness, begging her
to fold the veil over her breasts. I scrutinized
each scene, encounters where men talked and
women listened, faces molded at my fancy,
shuffled in my dreams, in every page I'd read.

Farewell to the shepherdess, leaning against
a horizontal trunk, chewing on a long-stemmed
pâquerette, lost in rapture at the shepherd's
speech. Her opulent breasts, freed from the
ruffled bodice, emerge, taunting as Caravaggio's
pears. He looks sideways, pointing
an index finger, half-smiling, seduced
by his own words, lascivious eyes oblivious
to the flock fleeing the canvas.
"She's looking for trouble," I often thought.
"Did it take long," I later asked, "to make
her skin so real?" "I don't remember," you
said, "but aren't her nipples *une petite
merveille*?" Schooled in a convent, you
chose to paint tender, playful scenes, always
telling your daughters: "Beware, never let
a boy kiss you," warning of hidden perils,
the paintings above our heads, teasing us silently.

*   *   *

Two women, face to face, facing palettes,
our dreams reshape spaces, erase corners,
stretch walls, fill oceans of absences. I watch you
run rivulets through rocky shores, wildflowers
springing while your mouth creases, a reflection
of your mother's pensive twitch as she pondered
the last notes of the Solitaire's decree.

Two girls read under a willow, faces receding,
more distant every day. "Here," I say, "let me
finish it." Mouth twisting, I bring the girls
to life. "I gave you my eyes," you said, that
day, smiling across the kitchen table, "I can
still paint Corot's landscapes."

Your late seasons revive in mine, against
the current, into your own. You guided my first
steps, the movements of the needle, the pen,
the brush. Now you play Solitaire, your hands
bring cards to wide-open eyes, hold magnifiers,
Psyche, immersed in endless tasks, too many
seasons bent over the easel, feathers, leaves,
flowers, emerged in silk, linen, wool, invaded
glass, wood, pewter, my daughter's smock,
until your root lost moisture.

Seated next to me, all eyes, the palm of your
hands, your fingertips, your empty, absent look,
follow my progress. I wear glasses now.
The sunset over the russet field defies me.
From above the columns of Solitaire, a voice
reaches my canvas: "Try a dry brush, a dash of
color, a drop of linseed oil."

The same smile sips Turkish coffee, turns cups
upside down. I read the dregs, you shuffle the pack.

Mobilis in Mobili

Watch how some people seem to be taking notes, but if we look closely, their pens race over the page, tracing cuneiform characters, arabesques, spirals intertwined in wildest vines, mysterious glyphs, oftentimes starting with a square or a circle they will randomly fill with parallel lines or curves, until the figure grows into a Rorschach stain in which they discover the extent—or limits—of their talent. And now that words refuse to follow the rows assigned to them, demand a life of their own, I find myself scribbling in concentric circles as if I were an insect lost inside a rosebud whirling like a dervish caught in a jinn's bottle until a flower emerges from the wraps and folds of his flying gown, his bent head a dark pistil deep inside a convolvulus and does it matter if it is not an arum or a delphinium?

I add more petals opening their wings, then a stem growing into a stalk, but it is closer to a bird standing on one foot, a cormorant, maybe, or a seagull, and with a few more feathers an Aztec headdress begs for a face, but I need not decide if it will wear a jaguar mask or bear a shield, I will fill empty spaces, erase borders, remapping my colonized realm until a boat emerges calling for a prow, a triangle for a mast, its sails ready to swell, billowing with the whim of the winds and a slight twist of the pen, almost floating on the tip of the white foam breaking into droplets over the glistening ship as if stopped in motion, a *mobilis in mobili*, until I can feel the mist over my face and around me the pull of the waves reaching me inside the captain's cabin where I am all alone bent over folds of maps, feeling the drift of the current guiding my pen as it slides along the mahogany desk, dragging me down over the wavering wooden floor.

Simulacra

At sunset, evading the canvas, her weary brush
  rests, inert, a broken stem.
    Drawn to the stream's silent
  murmur, she watches lines of liquid light encircle white
boulders, tremble into a mosaic of reflections.

The painter sits still, loosens her bow, wishes
  she'd lie on the riverbed,
    water running like fingers
  through her hair, the way the undercurrent combs
long wavering algae, willowing over rippled sand.

At a distance, passing clouds delineate black
  naked branches, heavy
    with birds like berries.
  She thinks of paper, pen and ink, reaches for her nearby
portfolio leaning against the abandoned

easel. Unable to move, her hair, entangled with
  mossy filaments, flows
    through crystalline
  waters. Reclined, she sees the birds fly,
clouds disappear as night falls over the creek.

Waves

He named her Ondine after a water nymph
who forgot
how to swim.
Carried away
by the current, she drowned in a dream.

Hours long she'd wait for him, watch
herons wade,
unexpectedly
spreading their wings
in flight, gliding on the breeze.

Anchoring herself to the illusion,
to a moment,
lights, shapes,
disappearing
she'd become water, a cold blue flame
he'd endlessly reinvent with his touch.

Blue Heron

An Egyptian sculpture
lost in the Northern wilderness,
the blue heron stands out
in the whitened landscape,
mimics an ibis' fixed stare,
studies the frozen creek,
sensing trembling gills
beneath the transparent sheet.

But why land in my backyard
I wonder, where no lotus ever grows?
Unless he sees his own ancestral roots
in my wide-open eyes lined with kohl,
and knows that water from the Nile
still runs in my veins since birth.

In warmer seasons he has seen me
feed the silver fish,
tend the vegetable garden,
bend over perennials
springing stronger each year,
add more seeds,
making this our home,
where we've lived the longest ever.

Today he saw me walk in circles
in the stillness of barren trees
over crisp snow flakes
masking all signs of life,
the forget-me-nots throbbing
under their icy coat, scintillating,

a thousand suns
opening a dam of flowing memories
of sunnier shores
promises of blossoms to come

until suddenly, as if pulsated by an engine,
statuesque, the migrant bird deploys gigantic
wings, disappears through the dead branches.

The Bullfrog

Like a Mandarin,
staring at his silky reflection,
a Narcissus frog
seated on an Arrowhead leaf
thinks he is a yellow flower.
I watch him,
my own split image,
schizophrenic frog,
conscious of the Other in himself.

II

Tea in Heliopolis

Immured

I live in an underground house, in the flank of one of the pyramids
of Giza. I breathe heavily the enclosed air, so thick it rubs over
me. I think of the doomed priests of Egypt who were buried alive.

This house has a secret wing, I move in it like in a dry aquarium.
Crystal and pink marble chandeliers cast a faded light over the
damask *Louis Seize* chairs. I address the elegant seats as if I expect
an answer. I am amazed at the impeccable condition of the room.

Delicate tapestries and old oils cover its walls. Carrara pink
marble tables tiptoe over pastel Persian rugs. This part of the
house is never used. No one knows of its existence, not even the
maid.

I have a sleep-in maid—she has no face, like in Mexican muralist
paintings; she spends her time sweeping the floor, an automaton.
We work together incessantly. I see endless corridors, a maze of
rooms waiting to be cleaned.

There are no windows. No one knows the house and I exist.
I live only for the house, a victim of the Pharaohs' eternal curse.

That Day in Heliopolis

At the movies,
I'd nest my head in his jacket,
his voice would slow
my heartbeat.
"Don't be afraid,
it is not real."

We rode camels at the Pyramids.
At the Palmyra café, he put
Backgammon pawns in my palms.
Everyone complained,
"You're spoiling the little brat."

At school, they threw me
off the team that day.
I was useless, they said,
"What a baby," someone said.
"Leave her alone,
she's crying because
her father is dead."

I waited all day
to come back home.
I understood
the black dress,
the pale, thin lips,
the pink Salon glittering,
shining like a monstrance...

"Is it true what they said?
Isn't he coming back?"
The lips moved...

Tea in Heliopolis

Here we are, alone,
comfortably seated
in an old faded photograph.
You are young, pretty.
We drink tea
like two old friends.

Two women, the same age,
like sad widows
we stare at the walls
built to fit your gilded Console.

Baguettes edge your paintings
with antique patina.
For years, bent over your canvas,
your youth was all painted,
not lived.

You add a little boiling water
from the silver Samovar.
We know we've already lost
that moment.

You take me by the hand to
a Jeweler's shop,
offer me a bow
inlaid with pearls.
"It is lovely," you say.
I prefer an emerald crescent.

The White Brass Bed

I loved that silk nightgown
you folded under me, Nonna.
I must have been five or six,
it was right before
your accident.

You kept me with you that night.
"I'll take good care of her," you said.
Your white brass bed shone,
a boat with a silver prow.

I remember you tall, erect,
slipping the long gown
over my shoulders,
your arms around me
standing in the middle of the bed.

I was six when you fell
under the metro, in Heliopolis.
Returning from the Palmyra café,
your skirt got caught in the door.
My older sister saw you slip
under the metallic wheels.

You live with us, Nonna.
You are always sitting,
you push the wheels
forward, backward,
one motion, both hands,
your only exercise.

You brought your bed along.
It is too high for you, now.
You sleep on a couch in a corner.
The white brass bed stands
in the middle, empty, useless.

I sleep in your bed, Nonna.
In my warm flannel, I feel
the softness of your silk nightgown.

Camera Lucida

The Chair she sat in, like a burnished throne,
Glowed on the marble.

—T. S. Eliot, *The Wasteland*

In her shimmering *déshabillé*,
she sits on a satin ottoman
facing the threefold image
of a young girl,

prey of two beauticians
busy with the last touches
of eye shadow and mascara.

They pull her long black hair,
securing it with forked pins,
preparing the insertion of
the headpiece.

She looks in the mirror,
expecting to be prettier,
happier than usual.
She closes her eyes.

Left alone, her hand smoothes
the muslin dress spread on the bed,
a white fan gathered
in the tight guipure bodice.

Under the silk ruffles,
her silver shoes emerge,
a twin net of glistening chain mail.
She retraces her steps to the altar.

She had called him, feeling cold.
He laughed, said it brought bad
luck to meet the day before.

She looks again at the girls
in the mirror as they raise
their hands to lower the veil.

Transience

A Sunday morning at the Crystal café,
I picture a child on the terrace,
a slender woman by her side,
her restless feet that once were mine,
circle around
a dome-shaped aviary glittering

like the Basilica's altar. Attentive
to the birds' motion,
she stops at times, palms resting
over golden bars
as wings on a screen.
Her dark eyes contemplate
the cloud masking
the sandy bottom. Small fingers
fumble through gilded
openings, pull fine,
silky feathers one by one.

I follow her home. Her red sandals
barely touch the ground.
One hand nestles
in the woman's,
another in her organdy smock.
In the secrecy of her room
she releases
a fluffy harvest
of blue-green dandelions
inside a scented Havana box.

An Indian Summer day, I imagine
her by my side, in Michigan.
Beneath the oaks,
inner branches suffuse a purple
glow. She thinks of makeup
thrown pell-mell
across her mother's dresser.
I help her gather leaves,
tender ocherous corals.

A gust of wind uncovers
tatters of flame.
I watch her pick transparent shades
one by one, press them between
her palms.
Sudden as a flap,
her laughter bursts, scattering feathers
over the green grass.

Waiting for Marie

Uneasy on a *Louis Seize* chair,
he crosses his legs,
waits for Marie and her daughter
to come through the beveled glass doors.

His eyes follow the navy-blue
arabesques of the pink Kashan carpet.
After forty years in America,
it felt good to read again
the language of oriental rugs.

He used to imagine
stories about stylized trees,
falcons and gazelles.
Marie and his sister were
friends then.

Once, he passed by the Groppi café,
offered the two girls *profiteroles.*

A voice startles him,
"Won't you sit in the *bergère,*
you'll be more comfortable.
How do you take your coffee?"

He sips the thick Turkish coffee,
looks at the middle-aged woman.
There was a likeness,
but where was Marie's elegance?

"I have been widowed a few years
now," she says. "I can't complain,
I've had some good years.
Mother was a widow too young."

"A chocolate," she says, holding
a blue Sèvres *bonbonnière*,
lid half-opened.

He'd sent her a porcelain *bonbonnière*.
It was a Capodimonte.
Little cupids were hanging
purple grapes on a garland.
He knew she'd like it.

She sent the box back.
He never saw her again.

"My mother has been
avoiding visits
since her accident,"
continues the voice.

Shut in her room,
an old woman in a wheelchair
prays he'll leave soon.
Her fifteen year-old heart
tight in a cocoon,
she hides her face in both hands
as if his eyes
could see
through walls.

Waiting in a Field of Melted Honey

I am waiting in a field of melted honey, hiding behind a blue tree that is not really a tree, a root Vincent chose to paint as a tree, you know, the painting where roots are the size of trees, gnarled trees with severed limbs, sterile against the golden field swaying, the tall grass bending, and of course no one can tell, but l feel the wind too, swelling my blue-flowered dress, you won't see none of it, for I am behind the huge roots that look like trees and you can only feel the wind in the brush strokes. You will mistake my dress bulging on the side for a knot as if I were a distortion of the oversized joints, leaning against the bark as if against one of his fingers, my space so restricted I can barely move.

The master knows I am waiting for him, eyes filled with the beauty pouring from his vision. I know he will take these roots and me with them, trees growing into rising clouds at nightfall, and he will show me the city lights everything around us becoming waves of light. When he remembers me, the tip of his brush releasing me, I will tell him how hot it was behind the root that was like a tree, how the bright rays made me dizzy. He will take me into his brush, cool me down with linseed oil and in another field show me the evening sky. I come to life again, but no one knows I'm here, the gold of my hair, the blue of my dress broken into lines, narrow paths of color spiraling among the stars on a warm blue night, the moon and the sun becoming one and I and him, the field and the sky circling endlessly. I feel the ripples of the wind, the ocean's foam, my dress flows domelike, its flowers brighter and brighter, I am everywhere, hear our voices and you now understand what lies in each swirl, your life, mine, his, together in the dance of the stars.

Amber Daum

An opalescent Daum vase placed on a pedestal in a lighted corner,
its wider base covered with overlapping silver vine leaves from which
it rose like a tree trunk, translucent as a vertical flame under sunlight.
Carved into crystal, a silvery leafed elm trapped like an insect or a
mote of dust inside amber resin, a tree within a tree-shaped vase.
One could almost feel the wind blowing through its dark veined
branches, sense the rustle of leaves that would never fall, flying like
petals as in Corot's landscapes, the same landscapes mother loved to
reproduce, bent hours long over an easel till she'd enter the scene.
Her brush would rearrange dot by dot the red scarf of the woman
resting under the arching elm in Mortefontaine, highlight with one
stroke the cap of the boatman anchoring his skiff alongside the
riverbank.

Your Name Was Also Mary

Head bent
over joined fists
you pray.
Knotted fingers
roll a bead,
stop for a Hail Mary.
Your whispers
echo the cicadas'
in neighboring
pines, while your
breath warms
the mother of pearls.

A gray
crocheted shawl
protects
your head, frames
your eyes and chin.
The rosary,
stretched between
clasped hands,
slides with litanies.

In the dark corridor
leading
to the bedrooms,
your Greek Icon
rests
in a niche,
lit by an oil lamp.

Mary's sad eyes
smile
in the thin flame.
You glide here
every day,
in your wheelchair
when the house
is silent.

The flame trembles
over walls,
your sinewy hands
and face,
like evening ripples,
resting rays
over drying
Mediterranean figs.

Your shadow,
a truncated pyramid
suddenly prays,
open hands raised,
you nod,
shake your head,
mumble words
you alone understand.

Eyes half-closed,
you stare
at the youthful face,
an oblique gaze
wanders about the image,
as moonlight
through lowered blinds.

A widow at twenty-one,
your life,
a succession of rosaries.

Open-Air Cinema in Heliopolis

You used to say, mother:
"Let me see your face when lit
by a crescent moon:
every day of the month
will smile the way you do."

We saw double-feature movies
in open-air theatres.
The cool breeze ran through our hair,
over our necks, lifted our skirts,
swayed us in a magical carpet.

Tempted by vendors chanting
Greek cheese and sesame breads,
we often stayed, sipping icy lemon
granitas through replays, the lift
and pause of cascading light.

Characters entered our own
camera obscura.
We never agreed on their age:
you added a few years,
I wanted them closer to mine.

I remember a recurrent scene,
fading now into a sepia cameo,
where a woman—always the same
yet different—slaps a man
before falling in his arms.

I watched your face then,
as stars outlined the sky,
the slight opening of the lips,
the Gioconda's elegant smile

you allowed yourself,
befitting the *sfumato* of the late hours.

Arm in arm, we walked home,
following the trail of the moon.

Everything They Said

All eyes, searching for hidden
treasures behind closed doors,
I'd climb and crawl like a ferret,
until I dug out from a linen
closet pictures of naked
women with painted smiles.

When you'd come home, we'd
play leapfrog, pretend we were
the same size, you'd kneel, see
the world at the level of my eyes.
You, tall warrior, bending
like a folded Ace, made the child
your Queen of Hearts.

When I was sick I slept
in the double bed covered with pink
satin. Sunlight filtered through ivory
lace, revealing tightly knotted
pastoral scenes. I counted docile sheep,
rested, lulled by cupid's harps and oboes.

At noon, you'd bring a pile of books,
I'd forget the white lace, lured
by the glossy pages. Later,
you'd appear, sipping the last drop
of Turkish coffee:
"Which one will you keep?"
"I read them all," I'd say. I knew
there'd be more at dinnertime.

Those days of symmetry,
everything counted double. Faces,
smiles, heavily outlined, stood
out, the way I edged the contours
of my drawings, wetting colored pencils
on the tip of my tongue.

At the movies, we once saw Rita
Hayworth perform Salome's dance
of seven veils. Back home, wrapped
in mother's silk scarves, like a top,
I spun, mimicking her. You both
laughed. "She's worth her weight
in gold," you said.

One January evening,
faces became flat, sketchy. I lived
inside a picture book, silhouettes
revolved around me from a distance,
beyond touch, unreal.

You wouldn't play that night. A hand
on your chest like a knight wounded
in battle, you said: "It's nothing,
Henriette, we'll go to the late show.
I am going to take a nap."

They brought you tea, a handkerchief
soaked in Atkinson Cologne.
Kneeling on your bed, in my flannel
pajama, I held the cold linen
against your burning forehead.
The pink bedspread was rolled like discarded bark.

Pulled away by strong arms, I saw
the doctor, the black case, the pinched lips,
the injection. From my room I peeked
through dark corridors: my mother seated
by the phone, the receiver in her clasped
hand, her face masked
by twisted, enormous fingers.

The next morning, I was taken away
from the silent house. "Your dad
is in the hospital," they said...

Forty years later, I still recall that long
January day at uncle Nicholas' villa.
My three younger cousins following me
from garden to greenhouse,
playroom to den, begging for stories.
Seated on the grass, holding a Bougainvillea
branch, my magic wand, I told them
my own version of Alice's misfortunes.
They believed everything I said.

12 Rushdy Street

At night, filtered by closed shutters
  ladders of light danced over my bedroom ceiling,
          neon streetlights,
headlights
  flooding walls with elusive shadows.

The soundtrack of the midnight *soirée*
  ascended from the nearby Riviera open-air cinema.

        Summer reruns, old familiar tunes,
                musical vines climb the balustrade
    finding their way through
wrought-iron fences woven with honeysuckle,

        the scent of jasmine rising, each waft of cool air
erasing the memory of scorching sun.

  Some in the house must have tossed around
helpless, buried their faces in pillows, while

I lay awake watching the incessant flicker,
          conjuring up lips half-open, eyelids
    lowered, I filled the blanks,
rewrote scripts,
      giving myself the best parts in the shadow play.

I grew a slim silhouette, long hair flowing
          in the wind over my shoulders
          on my first date,
    even rehearsed my wedding night
making sure
      every erotic scene was blessed by a sacrament
in view of the weekly confession.

First Bra

I remember when I turned eleven how my mother panicked: "Your cousin Coco is nine and has already lemon-sized breasts!" I didn't think lemons were pretty sprouting on one's chest but Coco's lemons were her mother's pride and my mother's despair.

I can still see the shimmer of my first bra, whose sole purpose was to maintain hope for better days as an amulet in fertility rites or a conjurer of seasonal rains.

Its layers of sheer nylon made me shiver when I'd feel them sliver between my fingers. I'd wash it with great care using soft soap foam as though its airiness carried arcane messages yet to decipher while I wore it against my flesh.

In French, *soutien-gorge* means support for the chest, or throat. That must be why my voice became hoarse every time I slipped it underneath my clothes.

Raindrops

It pours over rooftops,
against the walls
of my dreams. I rest
in Nonna's white brass
bed where I often lay,
feverish. In her wheelchair,
she circles, tucking
the embroidered linen
on both sides; her slender,
knotted hands, feathers,
erasing the distance
from her lips to my forehead.
Did she give birth in this
now vacant space,
inaccessible
to her useless legs?

Electrifying shears tear
the heavy night. I hear
my mother's voice:
"It rained relentlessly
when you were born.
I could not tell day
from night when I held
you in my arms."
Windshields fight droplets
of cold sweat in streets
shining like moist skins.
Egypt's sky forever blue,
except that day,
in Heliopolis,
when you held me
for the first time.

I think of us born
in Nonna's linen, of her
firm, soothing hand
on your forehead, raindrops,
marking the long hours.
I remember my children's
birth, the cold hospital bed,
the glistening shape
fleshed out of my pain,
your hands in mine.

I imagine us together,
both the same age,
mixing sighs, a rhythmical
throbbing rushing
through gutters,
against windowpanes.
I coil into your belly,
nestle in your arms.
And the piercing rain,
an omen, wilder than African
drums, beating our outstretched
skin, penetrates our hearts,
pinning us, wings wide-open,
over the white brass bed.

III

Raoucheh

Raoucheh,

Thirty-five years later, Beirut's Pigeons' Rock
forever mute witness of the civil war

a huge rock erect
   where purple evenings
        conjure Phoenician sails,
a backdrop to tales heard
  as a child, of lovers hiding,
       often drowning in its grotto's
emerald tears.
  I used to imagine
      how the Champollion,
          a ship venturing too close,
  lay trapped for years
    in blue mist,
        her insides
torn apart by this Giant's
  unclenched fist,
     stopped in slow motion,
        in an idle attempt to rise,
petrified by salt spray,
  her remains buried
    in quicksand
       in the midst of the Bay.

A fallen Olympian,
  forever flanked
     by dancing waves,
its ire, our inner
  obscure well, as if
     casting a black
        cloud over the former
brightness of sails,
  rustling canopies,
    over our steps along
the *Promenade des Français,*

breeze flowing
            through my curls, gusts
of wind sculpting
        our bodies, redesigning
            silhouettes,
erasing footsteps,
    echoes of laughter,
        muffled sighs,
            all the people
                    long gone.

Some, as pawns
    on a map, glided to
            another turquoise Bay,
                in Jounieh,
along the wavering coastline,
        an ersatz, surviving its artifice...
There, people of the same faith
            pull on the *narguilehs*
                in the cafés,
play dice and backgammon,

    women of the same clan
            stretch their smooth,
                lustrous bodies
        under the midday sun
deserting *Raoucheh*'s corniche
            its rocky shores now crowded
        only by male bathers
and fishermen,

while the imposing stone horseshoe
              clamped in indigo
    is no longer a good omen
after so many years
              of fallen,
                            dismantled bodies
    blown up theaters,
              casinos, snipers' crossfire
from deserted terraces,
    the air still remembers
              the smell of fear
                     and gunpowder,

its acrid taste unmasked
    by the unrelenting fumes
              of daily exhausts.
              In every corner,
    next to a restored building,
              an old house stands, scarred,
windowless,
              phantomlike,
    awaiting mouth agape
              the miraculous facelift.
The burning sun tires
    of recycling endless debris
              left over by thousands,
                     the waste of hatred,
    and time, once a healer
              broods despair.

Some far away will dream
  a laced balcony,
        delicate mosaics, unfaded,
  patina adding its final touch
        to pink façades, sepia walls
faceted stones,
  deeply engraved in the retina
        unfolding in the mirrors
              of our minds.

I recall how wafts of orange blossoms
        mixed with effluvia
              of salty breeze,
  once whispering under pillars
        and arcades, would reach us
as we rested under a Jacaranda's
  trembling blue shade.

I often gazed through thick glass,
  at the delicate displays of vials and flasks
        rescued from the depths
              of Tyre and Sidon
gilded by time,
  marveled at the fluidity of erosion
        over blown glass
              and burnished metals,
all pearl-like treasures forever gone,

  like so many of us,
        the lucky ones
fading away in distant lands
  dreaming new dreams,
        our children unaware
of what is no longer there,
  unable to hear the voices
        we cannot silence

the song of the orphans
the song of the fishermen's nets
the song of the abandoned house
the song of the goat living in a palace
the song of the refugees milking a goat over Persian carpets
the song of the windshields constellated with stars of death
the song of the driver forced to leave his car at an intersection
the song of an entire school bus emasculated because they were Maronites
the song of mothers and children blown up because they were not Maronites
the song of a town torn apart, its children hanging like heavy fruits from olive
    and almond-trees, nipples and testicles dripping with blood on the
    lower branches
the song still heard through murmuring leaves, cacti and pine needles,
    as the roots remember
the song of Beirut burning us safe watching the flames from a hill,
    waiting for the madness to reach the mountains
the song of the man who never returned home, his head rolling behind his car
the song of a fool who crossed the green line to meet his Muslim lover,
    only to be found the next day in a small bag under the infamous bridge
the song of the silent ride over the bridge of death, the only way to the airport.
I ran to have a passport picture taken with the two of you,
    tried to comb your hair as best as I could.
Your hair so fine, it curled around my fingers.

IV

A Glimpse of Fall

Encounters

In the tower of a restored Italian cloister a bourgeois restaurant
flourishes in its loggias I meet the high dignitaries of my adventures
my djinns and afrits

We're trapped in the basement of a building in Beirut with many
unknown families we'll have to cross the street at dawn
to change shelter during the next truce

In a car parked in a dark alley a hand slowly outlines my eyes
the bridge of my nose lingers at my lips and neck
everyone hears my heartbeat

Alone in my bed again crying I hit with my fists the indifferent wall

On an indefinite sheet of water surrounded by two lines of rowers
she watches the rhythmic synchronized movements
of their gigantic oar
the boat barely touches the surface

Your smile tells me in a stairwell "You haven't changed in twenty
years you stood it all well"

it's getting harder to sit i become heavier every day i'm no longer
good for anything anymore i'd like a small drop to warm
my heart up children bring my shawl please

We walked hand in hand over brittle pine needles wild oregano
in bloom thorny umbels swarming with shiny ants

its impossible my house isn't for sale i'll never sell

Adagio for a Forgotten *Viola d'Amore*

> *...hyperspace may provide a means*
> *to tunnel through space and time...*
> —Michio Kaku

In the dark corner
        of an abandoned attic
     I found a *Viola d'amore*
        leaning against a rocking chair

        the only seat that kept my back
    straight when pregnant,
      mute companion
of long waking hours

 It was a chair I thought I'd use
      now that my back aches with age

      And how important was this rocking chair
        when we lost it all in Beirut?

        The chair was in the attic
    I visited in my dream
      a *Viola d'amore* leaning over it

     its back as straight as the chair's
a few strings loose

        And topping its long neck
    a carved cupid's head
so covered with dust
      you could never have guessed
        it was blindfolded

Does it really matter that no one ever played in the family?

Only what the carved head
        overheard whenever pressed
            firmly under the chin
        of the slender girl

          when she was young and strong
     not yet my Nonna
sliding through corridors
        in a wheelchair

I wonder how she played then
      in the balcony
          of our house in Heliopolis
or was it Alexandria?

I can see her pull the flat body
      against her chest
         each unbowed note

       She had a way of walking
    that caught the eye
until she married
      at sixteen
   to a jeweler freemason
who knew nothing about music

That's when she placed her *Viola* in the attic
     next to my rocking chair

A Glimpse of Fall

My Art teacher says,
"Never paint a tree
in Spring or Summer,
paint them nude,
when you can see them
embrace each other,
when their antlered arms
raise in different directions."

It's too cold to paint
outdoors where the river
begins to melt under
ducks' emerald green.

I'm glad the next-door
neighbors didn't build.
Their tall crackled oaks
will be mine a while longer
still covered with
shriveled sandy-ochre leaves.

Leaves dry, cling
to their old birthplace.
I think of my mother
who always wanted
to be buried in Egypt
beside her husband, mother,
in their family vault.
Now, she'll be buried
in the New World.

When I'd tell her,
"I'm taller than you
now," she'd say,
"Don't you know people
shrink with age? I wasn't
always like this."

I try to pull the crisp
auburn leaves, one by one.
They look old, dead,
but alive inside.
They won't give up
until a new leaf
pushes them aside.

It Was Later on I Learned It Was Harmless

Pulling weeds next
to my purple rhododendrons,
I saw the snake right
by my doorstep. I mean,
it could have easily slipped
into the house. It disappeared
under myrtle and lavender
blooms, hiding in dark corners
edged with slippery leaves,
seeking the coolness
of humus. I ran for a shovel,
aimed, imagining I would split
it in two. A clean job.
I had seen butchers chop ribs
with a sharp knife. I'd give
it a merciful blow. I saw its jaw
open in agony, its dislocated body
still holding together, flesh visible
under flayed skin, uncovered bowels
shone in broad daylight, eyes
disappearing into a button hole,
it still wriggled ...
I hit and hit again, metal sliding
against scales, shivering
all over, I hit harder, thought
of brothers face to face, limbs
severed, the madness. I couldn't stop.
I tried to find a reason to finish
the job. I kept telling myself:
it does not feel anything, I'd be
too scared to work in the yard.
I had no choice. I had to do it.

The Road to Tyre

spreads its loose ribbon along the shoreline,
through orange groves hedged with white jasmine...

"We'll stop at Sidon,"
you once said, "I'll tell you
the secrets of every stone,
of every carving. We'll bring
back a blue vase
of iridescent blown-glass,
perhaps a small *narguileh.*"

On the roadside, an old peasant
wearing a white shirt
and gathered black pants
leads a donkey
loaded with fruit baskets.

"I'd like to buy pomegranates
to share when we return
to Beirut," I thought.
"I'll part the red leathered
skin, roll the ruby seeds
beneath my fingers
one by one."

I can still feel the salty breeze
on my lips, the warm,
dizzying scent of orange
blossoms, a bridesmaid's
endless walk to the altar.

We never made it to Tyre
that day.
We never saw the Crusaders'
Castle together,
we'll never cross its paved
causeway hand in hand,
a narrow path, invisible
from a distance,
like a carpet thrown over
the blue waters, linking
its threshold to the shore.

Year after year
we dreamt of going South
again. The pomegranates
untouched,
forgotten on a shelf
receded in my mind,
they must have shriveled
like the fruits I pick
with care, then throw
out the window, deep
into woods.

The Wheel

It is a small apartment
on a rooftop overlooking
a Merry go Round,
and a big lighted Wheel
by the sea cornice,
lined with palm trees.
You check several closets
filled with your children's
clothes, soft woolens and cotton
knits that never touched their skin,
toys they never played
with, you know,
the ones you saved
on the higher shelves,
scented with lavender
for when they're older.
Someone lives there, an old
Lebanese who signals more
doors replete with boxes
marked with your initials.
He can't return any.
Then, you realize these closets
are hidden somewhere
in the back of your mind.
You're just too busy
to open them.

Narguileh

Trapped in his backyard,
an old man
thinks of cafés,
backgammon games, dice
thrown over inlaid wood.
Fingertips folded
on an empty palm, hand
recapturing the lost motion,
he draws on his pipe,
reviving crackling embers,
attentive to the divas' deep
vibrato, Feyrouz,
Sabah, Om
Kolsoum.

He breeds canaries
in a shed, feeds them egg
shells, slices of apple.
Each dawn, he hangs
cages on the trellis
overlooking the swing,
waters his vegetables,
precious seeds
flown from far away,
curled cucumbers,
a special vine from Lebanon,
its silken leaves
fit for stuffing.

Rolling patience beads
made of coral,
he sits for hours
under the covered porch.
Lips stuck to the tip
of the painted pipe,
he thanks the Lord
his grandchildren
will live free
in the New World.
Does it matter if
his soul sinks
in an iridescent flask
blown into eddies of smoke?
Eastern voices mix
with the birds' song, Sabah,
Om Kolsoum,
Feyrouz.

Carefully kindling coals
with tongs, he watches
arabesques, swirls emerging
from underwater, imprisoned
in the blown glass,
bursting at the surface,
deafened words
of a drowned Phoenician sailor.

Even the Sun Has Its Dark Side

but does it really matter,
            unless
we could enter that hidden space,
            the way grains of sand
                    would suddenly rise
in an hourglass,
            reshape themselves,
            regain their initial place.
I wonder what is lost behind a picture,
            rippled in its negative
as I often try to read between the lines,
            sense clenched teeth,
                    or grasp an unspoken word.

When I set to bridge these gaps,
my blood warms up in tides,
            revealing a tightness inside the chest
                    as if memories,
            pressed in a tin can
            kept near one's heart,
could sweep away the grayness outside.

We lost everything when we fled,
except for an album
            full of my childhood pictures in Egypt
            and my children born in Beirut.
"You're so lucky," everyone said,
            our family unharmed,
                    not one of their fingers
                    was worth the whole world
left behind.

Our beds were made in places
where the sun teased us, hiding
most of the time, forcing us to master
the local motto
...make sunshine inside...
Christmases followed one another
offering versions of our lives,
each fragmented image
evoking a new face,
a recipe ...an absence...

Whenever I sort them out,
I see myself floating in a fluid
lining edges
in search of a referent that has vanished,
leaving only an empty shell,
crumpled, discolored like fallen leaves.

I felt constantly renewed,
peeled off like an onion,
shedding layer after layer
until what was left
was so tender,
une primeur à déguster,
yet so vulnerable.

Black and White Photographs

the repotted bulb spread roots
        in the New World's moist soil
wings grew
             like praying hands
     in different tongues
overlapping its core
      to mend what was undone,
           until it looked whole again

children rebelled against
      whatever came from a distant land,
and year after year we learned
to sit in front of the camera,
      gather a succession
          of perfect moments
till I lost track of what lies
      under these smiles.

How could I ever part
with my old black and white photographs,
    taken when I was a little girl
        and no one forced me to smile,
    yet I knew how loved I was... pictures
of my parents proudly seated in a mock airplane
about to take-off...
          ...my mother's delicate lace net
          coming down her *toque*,
          half-covering her eyes, head
          slanted in an enigmatic look
         a la Garbo...my father in
         black tie and white scarf, a tall
         hat in his hand.

I see you posing with us, mother.
>   Your age, the same as mine,
playing a role,
>   a proud, perfect mother. Yet, I never saw
you happy, I mean really...
>   Nothing like our pictures, the four of us
radiant,
>   year after year.
>   I got used to smiling, you know, thought it
made me look younger,
>   helped hide the wrinkles.
After capturing the sun inside me,
>   now the peer pressure...
>   ...the need for American Beauty.

To My Son Upon His First Visit to Lebanon

He wanted to see our summerhouse
   in the mountains of Baabdat,
enter the pictures
     where a young woman his age,
   her long hair flowing in the wind,
guided his first steps on the terrace.
He wanted to dream in a language never learned,
   see himself reflected in familiar faces,
recapture smells and fragrances.

He finally saw the orchard his father planted
   tree after tree, green and black figs, cherries,
peaches, plums, pears, apples, almonds...
     One hundred fruit trees
   we would not see blossoming
     spring after spring.
   And the purple grape seeds from Japan,
the miniature green seedless *Banati* from Egypt,
   covering the trellis, tempting clusters
hanging low, cast shadows on the shaded patio.

The cut stone house, its tiled roof,
   seemed out of place.
     What ever happened
   to the one in the family album?
No longer surrounded by green mountain slopes,
nor an open view to the horizon.
   Erratic buildings sprouted like mushrooms
     during the civil war.
Concrete was biting the flanks of the mountains,
   spreading like a contagious disease.

He rang the doorbell.
The tenants were friendly, inviting him in.
   They said the present owner was very proud
of his orchard, that he himself
    had planted each one of these tall, imposing trees...
He called us excited, said he wanted to buy
   the house back.
      We could spend summers there.
Time regained, he thought...
   eager to relive our dream,
retrieve its lost broken pieces,

I tried to explain what does belonging *mean* exactly?
And does it really matter?

Lost and Found

This could be an office, a Temple or a church.
Its thick crimson carpeted floor
muffles all sounds
      as if we were walking over clouds.
Here people wait in line
drawn by an invisible cord.

Objects with a will of their own, call names,
conjure-up faces, find their way
on pre-labeled shelves,
uprooted lares and penates reappear,
faithful to their hosts...

Behind a counter, three matronly women
display heteroclite items:

> *a silver candle snuffer, a collection of thimbles, an enameled hand mirror*
> *inlaid with semi-precious stones, a crystal chandelier, brass engraved*
> *ashtrays and planters, an old gas Primus stove, a miniature locket, a*
> *silver samovar, a powder case covered with petit-point, an oval mahogany*
> *mantle clock, a jade Buddha, a copy of a pink lacquered lampshade with*
> *pewter cupids my mother carved when she was fifteen and even a deep-*
> *blue Sèvres porcelain bonbonnière—a Boucher's pastoral painted on its*
> *lid—similar to the one my father presented the day he proposed...*

My mother and I have come regularly for years,
crossing oceans or land,
we never fail to meet at the threshold
of the crimson corridor
      we still look the same we did thirty years ago,
            before the fighting started

Hand in hand, we wait in line,
talk as if we never parted, reviving
a once congealed image, a never-ending moment...

She hopes to recover her paintings,
or at least one, the Galleon or the Shepherdess
Perhaps this is what I'd like most to see,
                    her own work
"May evil come upon those who have them
on their walls," she says...

I'm afraid to go to someone's home in Lebanon
and see my life scattered all over,
                    fetishes sold at black markets
As if I owned a palace
As if it mattered
As if anything mattered
          since our children left
untouched, unharmed

Salawat

Lament of an old Lebanese.

I have lost count
of nights
lulling myself to sleep,
magical signs,
salawat, unheard
pleas,
my rosary,
restrung so many times,
I can no longer
distinguish
Ave from Gloria.
I could be imploring Allah,
my beads
the same size
as my neighbor Yasmine's
who lost
two sons.

All of us
people
of the Book,
all faithful, burned incense,
knelt
in the right direction,
all wept
at the wakes of loved ones.
Now, in each home
an oil lamp lights
black picture frames.
A flat stone
pressed
against my heart,
the used-up
words, eroding
the tip of our tongue,

our lips, our soul,
keep coming,
salawat,
soothing
like water falling
over
boulders.

HEDY HABRA was born in Egypt and is of Lebanese origin. She is the author of a short story collection, *Flying Carpets*, and a book of literary criticism, *Mundos alternos y artísticos en Vargas Llosa*. She has an MA and an MFA in English and an MA and PhD in Spanish literature, all from Western Michigan University, where she currently teaches. She is the recipient of WMU's All-University Research and Creative Scholar Award and a Doctoral Dissertation Completion Fellowship Award. She writes poetry and fiction in French, Spanish, and English and has more than 150 published poems and short stories in numerous journals and anthologies, including *Drunken Boat, Cutthroat, Nimrod, Puerto del Sol, The New York Quarterly, Cider Press Review, Poet Lore, Poetic Voices Without Borders 2, Inclined to Speak,* and *Dinarzad's Children* Second Edition. For more information, visit www.hedyhabra.com.

CPSIA information can be obtained at www.ICGtesting.com
Printed in the USA
BVOW020618270313

316580BV00002B/80/P